Poor Sam

by Kaye Umansky

THE CAST

SAM

MUM
(Jill Summerday)

DR PRICE

BEN

JOJO

MOUSE

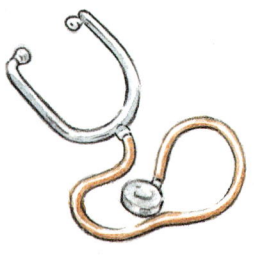

Scene 1

Sam's bedroom. Sam is in bed. Dr Price and Mum are with her.

MUM Oh dear. Chicken pox, you say?

DR PRICE Yes. Look at her spots.

SAM I feel all right. Can I go out to play?

DR PRICE Oh no, Sam. Not for two weeks.

SAM Two weeks? But what shall I do?

DR PRICE You must stay in and rest.

Sam groans.

MUM Poor Sam.

Scene 2

The street below Sam's flat.

Enter Ben, Mouse and Jojo.

BEN Did you hear? Sam is sick.

JOJO Her mum says it's chickenpox.

MOUSE Can we go to see her?

BEN No. We'll catch it too.

MOUSE Poor Sam. She'll be bored.

Sam appears on her balcony.

MOUSE Yoo-hoo! Sam!

JOJO She can't hear you.

Sam goes back into her bedroom.

BEN She has gone back in.

Sam comes out on to the balcony.

JOJO   Wait! There she is again.

BEN   What is she doing?

Sam lowers a basket tied to a long string.

MOUSE   She has tied a basket to some string!

JOJO   Here it comes.

MOUSE   There is a note.

JOJO   What does it say?

BEN   It says 'I AM BORED'.

JOJO   What can we do to help?

BEN   Come on. I have an idea.

All exit.

Scene 3

Sam's bedroom. Sam is in her dressing gown.

Enter Mum.

MUM How do you feel, Sam?

SAM Fed up.

MUM Poor old you.

SAM I don't like being ill.

MUM Do you want to read?

SAM I've read all my books.

MUM Do you want to make something?

SAM No. I'm too tired, Mum.

MUM What is that noise? I hear shouting.

Mum goes out onto the balcony.

Scene 4

The balcony.

MUM Sam! Come out here. Ben and Mouse and Jojo want you.

Sam joins her on the balcony. They look down.

MUM What are they shouting?

SAM I think they want me to let down the basket.

MUM What basket?

SAM This basket.

She lowers it.

MUM What a good idea!

SAM Coming up!

She pulls it up.

MUM What have you got?

Sam takes the things out, one by one.

SAM Lots of things. A comic and some stickers!

MUM Some new felt pens!

SAM Some sweets and a big, green apple!

MUM A puzzle book!

SAM And a note.

MUM What does it say?

SAM It says 'POOR SAM. GET WELL SOON'.

MUM How kind of them.

Scene 5

Ben, Mouse and Jojo wait on the street below.

JOJO I hope she likes the things.

MOUSE She's looking at them.

BEN She's waving to us.

JOJO Look! The basket is coming back down.

BEN There is a note in it.

JOJO I'll read it.

MOUSE What does it say?

JOJO It says 'THANK YOU FOR THE THINGS. LOVE, SAM'.

They all wave up to Sam.

Scene 6

Sam's bedroom. Two weeks later.

Enter Dr Price and Mum.

DR PRICE Hello, Sam. How do you feel?

SAM Hello, Dr Price. I feel fine.

DR PRICE Good. I see your spots have gone.

MUM Can she go out to play?

DR PRICE Yes. I think she can.

SAM Hooray! I'm going out now.

There is a crash as she trips over.

SAM OW!

The End